MW01126517

GROWTH MINDSET JOURNAL FOR GIRLS

This book is dedicated to

....
Write your name here

GROWTH MINDSET JOURNAL for Girls

A Space to Embrace Challenges,
Build Confidence, and Dream Big

Jamie Leigh Bassos, MS, BCBA

ROCKRIDGE
PRESS

Copyright © 2022 by Rockridge Press, Oakland, California

No part of this publication may be reproduced, stored in a retrieval system, or transmitted in any form or by any means, electronic, mechanical, photocopying, recording, scanning, or otherwise, except as permitted under Sections 107 or 108 of the 1976 United States Copyright Act, without the prior written permission of the Publisher. Requests to the Publisher for permission should be addressed to the Permissions Department, Rockridge Press, 1955 Broadway, Suite 400, Oakland, CA 94612.

Limit of Liability/Disclaimer of Warranty: The Publisher and the author make no representations or warranties with respect to the accuracy or completeness of the contents of this work and specifically disclaim all warranties, including without limitation warranties of fitness for a particular purpose. No warranty may be created or extended by sales or promotional materials. The advice and strategies contained herein may not be suitable for every situation. This work is sold with the understanding that the Publisher is not engaged in rendering medical, legal, or other professional advice or services. If professional assistance is required, the services of a competent professional person should be sought. Neither the Publisher nor the author shall be liable for damages arising herefrom. The fact that an individual, organization, or website is referred to in this work as a citation and/or potential source of further information does not mean that the author or the Publisher endorses the information the individual, organization, or website may provide or recommendations they/it may make. Further, readers should be aware that websites listed in this work may have changed or disappeared between when this work was written and when it is read.

For general information on our other products and services or to obtain technical support, please contact our Customer Care Department within the United States at (866) 744-2665, or outside the United States at (510) 253-0500.

Rockridge Press publishes its books in a variety of electronic and print formats. Some content that appears in print may not be available in electronic books, and vice versa.

TRADEMARKS: Rockridge Press and the Rockridge Press logo are trademarks or registered trademarks of Callisto Media Inc. and/or its affiliates, in the United States and other countries, and may not be used without written permission. All other trademarks are the property of their respective owners. Rockridge Press is not associated with any product or vendor mentioned in this book.

Interior and Cover Designer: Linda Kocur
Art Producer: Alyssa Williams
Editor: Jeanann Pannasch
Production Editor: Ruth Sakata Corley
Production Manager: Jose Olivera

Illustrations © Anugraha Design/Creative Market, except for the following icons: © Shutterstock.com, pp. 32, 50, 109, 123, 134.
Author photo courtesy of Oona Cruger.

Paperback ISBN: 978-1-63878-174-5
R0

CONTENTS

WELCOME TO YOUR JOURNAL

This is a safe space for any girl ready to take control of their future and success! No matter what's happening in your life right now, this journal is for *you*!

My name is Jamie Bassos, and I am a behavior analyst who has been working with kids just like you for over 20 years. I see lots of people with opinions on how we should look, behave, think, and feel. I am here to tell you to trust yourself. Don't be afraid to grow into whoever you feel you can be! Use this journal to help recognize your full potential. You'll come out a more confident, brave, and happy you!

WHAT IS GROWTH MINDSET?

Good news: You have incredible power! You *already* have the capacity to shape your mind and control your own success. All it takes is focusing on your mindset—or how you think.

When it comes to having a "mindset," there are two possible options: a fixed mindset and a growth mindset. A fixed mindset means you feel you were born with your intelligence, personality, and capabilities, and cannot change them. Because of this, you may avoid new experiences, and view your mistakes as failures instead of opportunities for growth and improvement. Maybe you want to learn to play basketball, for example, but think you can't play because you are not tall enough. A growth mindset (the one we are striving for) is when you believe your brainpower, skills, and talents can improve and get stronger with the right strategies. In this basketball example, you would confidently come up with strategies, such as training the right muscles and researching great on-court plays.

Girls are more likely than boys to have a fixed mindset, which is why this journal is designed just for you—to give *you* the power of a growth mindset. Here are eight basic growth mindset beliefs this journal will focus on:

1. Effort and hard work are the keys to success, not just talent.

2. Mistakes and failures help you learn.

3. Unhelpful thoughts limit you.

4. You can create positive thoughts.

5. Frustration is a normal part of growth.

6. Comparison can hold you back.

7. Feedback and criticism are important for change.

8. Change is good.

These beliefs reflect the themes you'll work through in the chapters ahead, equipping you with the tools necessary to be your best self!

HOW TO USE THIS JOURNAL

This journal is for you to use any way you want. Read it in one sitting, or pick it up whenever you are feeling emotions you want to explore. Keep it confidential, or share it with those you trust. This is your safe space to draw, write, doodle, and express yourself. The coolest part? There are *no* rules! No one is going to tell you the ways you *have* to use this space. There is no right or wrong way. This is a judgment-free zone, so allow yourself to mess up, try again, erase, cross out, and try again and again and again.

Use this journal to be brave and vulnerable. Maybe find a cozy place in your room or where you live to consistently sit when journaling. I like to listen to music when I write (I am listening right now!). Other people need a quiet space, alone and away from the rest of the world. Wherever you are comfortable, set up a time and space for yourself. Grab some pens, markers, pencils (colored or plain), glitter, and/or stickers, and let's get creative as we start this journey into that flexible, incredible mind of yours!

Your Amazing Mind

How well do you *really* know yourself? I am in my late 30s and am still getting to know myself! I learn something new about myself every day, because guess what? Even though I am an adult, I discover new things about who I am and who I want to be all the time. This first section will help you learn a lot about yourself: your own unique strengths, interests, passions, and goals. We are going to explore your mind and dig deep! Ready to get curious?

Love Yourself

Did you know that being your own best friend is harder than being a friend to someone else? We can be so critical of ourselves! We speak to ourselves in ways that we would never speak to a friend. Let's work on being kinder to ourselves.

What makes you *you*? Write three things that are unique to you and make you feel special.

1. ....

2. ....

3. ....

Write three things you are really good at. What makes you good at these things?

1. ....

2. ....

3. ....

Look at yourself in the mirror. What are four compliments a best friend would give you today?

1. ....

2. ....

3. ....

4. ....

When someone gives you a compliment, how do you typically respond? How does the compliment make you feel on the inside?

....

....

....

....

What is your hidden superpower? Write a sentence about something you can do that not too many people know about.

....

....

....

....

Write a list of things about yourself that you are most proud of; think of traits and skills, not just things you've done.

....

....

....

If you could change three things in your life that you feel are in the way of you being good at something, what would they be?

1. ....

2. ....

3. ....

What is something you are not good at right now and want to get better at?

....

....

....

....

Self-Love Checklist! Check off things that are TRUE for you *today.*

- ☐ When I look in the mirror, I like what I see.

- ☐ When someone gives me a compliment on something I did well, I feel good.

- ☐ I talk to myself like someone I love.

- ☐ I am loved by the people around me.

- ☐ When I am sad, I can feel those uncomfortable feelings.

- ☐ When I make a mistake, I can forgive myself and try again.

- ☐ When someone corrects me, I can accept it and look inward.

- ☐ I belong here.

If you were unable to check any of these, that is okay! I can promise you that by the end of this journal, you will be able to check off at least one.

"Love yourself first and everything else falls into line."

—Lucille Ball

Set Your S.M.A.R.T. Goals

Settings goals can be tricky. We don't want them to be too big, or too small, or too far in the future. We are going to practice writing **S.M.A.R.T.** goals.

- Specific
- Measurable
- Achievable
- Relevant
- Time-bound

List three things you want to learn how to do.

1. ....

2. ....

3. ....

Now, take those goals and turn them into **s**pecific, **m**easurable, **a**chievable, **r**elevant, and **t**ime-bound goals. For example: "I want to learn how to read music (relevant, specific) by the end of fourth grade (achievable, time-bound) so I can play piano in the school orchestra in fifth grade (measurable)."

....

....

List three things you want to learn to do better, or things you want to improve on.

1. ....

2. ....

3. ....

Now, make those goals **s**pecific, **m**easurable, **a**chievable, **r**elevant, and **t**ime-bound. For example, "I want to get a better grade (achievable) on my math test (relevant), by at least 10 points (specific, measurable), at the end of the next math section (time-bound)."

....

....

....

....

What can you do if some*thing* gets in your way and delays you from meeting one of your goals within your expected time frame?

....

....

....

....

If your expectations for yourself are not met as you work toward a goal, how can you be gentle with yourself (for instance, giving yourself a second chance)?

....

....

If some*one* gets in your way of meeting a goal, what are some ways you can be gentle with your reaction and response to them?

....

....

....

....

Self-advocating, or speaking up for yourself and communicating your needs, can support you in meeting your goals. What are some ways you feel comfortable speaking up for yourself (for example, privately telling an adult you need help)?

· ·

· ·

· ·

· ·

If you are not yet comfortable asking for help, what are some ways you can practice asking for help (for instance, writing a note or email to your parents instead of asking face-to-face)?

· ·

· ·

Lists can help you organize your thoughts. Pick one of the goals you wrote down on page 7. Make a to-do list of three to five things you may need to do to meet that goal. If you are unsure, ask for help!

1. ....

2. ....

3. ....

4. ....

5. ....

> "Decide what you want. Declare it to the world. See yourself winning."
>
> —Misty Copeland

Open Your Mind

Are you open to new experiences and people?
Everyone you meet can teach you something
new about yourself in one way or another.
You never know what their story can bring to
your life!

Close your eyes and open your mind. Think about a time you said *yes* to a new experience, even though you were nervous about it. What was it, and how did it make you feel?

· ·

· ·

· ·

Do you get excited about new ideas or experiences? What was the last new idea you got excited about?

· ·

· ·

· ·

Being able to reevaluate your own beliefs and ideas and rethink conclusions are important parts of a personal growth mindset. When was the last time someone told you something you didn't know or something that was different from your perspective? How did it cause you to rethink your opinion?

· ·

· ·

· ·

How do you feel when you change your mind after getting new information?

. . . .

. . . .

. . . .

. . . .

Think about one of your strong beliefs. How can you seek out information that challenges this belief in order to learn about a different perspective?

. . . .

. . . .

. . . .

. . . .

Is it easy for you to listen to or understand someone else's strong, emotional feeling without becoming emotional, too? Why or why not?

. . . .

. . . .

. . . .

. . . .

Do you think you are someone who truly wants to hear and listen to other people's points of view?

....

....

....

Setting aside judgment is key to being open-minded. What are three ways you can respond to others without using judgment?

1. ....

2. ....

3. ....

Confirmation bias is when you favor information that confirms your existing beliefs and ideas. Being open-minded can help you avoid this way of thinking. Think about a time you accepted information simply based on who was telling it to you. What questions can you ask next time?

....

....

....

If you are having a disagreement with someone, what is a kind way to "agree to disagree"?

....

....

....

....

"Life is not easy for any of us . . . We must have perseverance and above all confidence in ourselves. We must believe that we are gifted for something and that this thing must be attained."

—Marie Curie

Celebrate Your Brain Power!

Neuroplasticity is a fun word to say, and it is a fun thing to imagine. Close your eyes and picture your brain learning something new. When you try new things, and persevere through things that are challenging, your brain makes new connections and grows. The more times your brain makes these new connections, the more likely it is that your powerful brain muscle will remember and make these connections again. You literally grow your brain!

Remember a time when you tried a new food, skill, or sport you found super challenging. What was it? How did it feel?

....

....

....

....

Did you end up trying that challenging thing again? How did it feel the second, third, or fourth time you did it? Was it easier? How?

....

....

....

....

What are three new and challenging things you want to try next?

1. ....

2. ....

3. ....

Did you know that eating well can help improve your brain function and memory? Yum! What are some healthy food choices?

....

....

....

....

Fun fact: Singing and listening to music can help you learn new things. What are some of your favorite songs?

....

....

....

....

I like to move it, move it! Exercising can improve your mood and physical health, which also help your brain (and you!) feel happy. What are three physical activities or sports you enjoy?

1. ....

2. ....

3. ....

Laughing can improve memory and overall mood. What is your favorite joke, or something that made you laugh really hard this week?

....

....

....

Sharing is caring! Connecting with others helps regulate emotions and build greater empathy for others. What is a funny story you would like to tell your friends or family about?

....

....

....

Feeling sleepy? Getting enough sleep helps your memory. It can also help your brain solve problems. What is your bedtime, and how many hours of sleep do you usually get each night? Could you use more sleep?

....

....

....

....

What calms you down at night and helps you get ready to sleep? What do you do to get comfortable and ready for bed?

....

....

....

....

"You may not control all the events that happen to you, but you can decide not to be reduced by them."

—Maya Angelou

Get Curious!

Sometimes, a growth mindset starts with curiosity. Have you ever wondered what is attracting you to a certain person, place, activity, or thing? Or wondered why this new thing, all of a sudden, is so interesting? These are signals to dig deeper and continue asking questions.

What has been attracting your interest lately?

....

....

....

....

What about it is so interesting or intriguing to you?

....

....

....

....

List three questions you have about this interest.

1. ....

2. ....

3. ....

Now think about someone who may know about that thing or topic. What questions can you ask them about it?

....

....

....

....

Think of a person you would like to get to know better. What are three questions you can ask them about themselves?

1. ....

2. ....

3. ....

New people are also curious about *you*! What three things would you want to share with someone you haven't met yet so they can get to know you better?

1. ....

2. ....

3. ....

If you had a crystal ball that could see into the future, what is one question you would ask?

....

....

....

....

Why would you ask your crystal ball that question?

....

....

....

....

If you could be an expert on anything in the world, what would it be? Why?

....

....

....

....

How would you go about becoming such an expert?

....

....

....

....

"Don't let anyone rob you of your imagination, your creativity, or your curiosity. It's your place in the world; it's your life. Go on and do all you can with it, and make it the life you want to live."

—Mae C. Jemison

Challenge Yourself!

In the statement pairs below, which one represents a growth mindset?

a. I am not good at this.

b. I can be good at this with time and practice.

a. My friend doesn't like the color of my shirt, so I went home and changed.

b. My friend doesn't like the color of my shirt, so I told her that I do, and that wearing it makes me feel good.

a. I tried something hard today and didn't give up when I failed.

b. I tried something hard today and gave up after my first mistake.

a. I don't like the way any of my clothes feel or fit me.

b. I love the way I look and feel in this outfit!

Answers: b, b, a, b

How did you do? It's okay if you got some answers wrong, because you are here, working on your growth mindset! The answers will come easier as you progress through your journal.

Challenge Yourself

The next time you get some new information, keep the following questions in mind:

☐ What facts do I know about this topic already?

☐ How much does the person telling me this information know about this topic, and where did they get their information?

☐ Have I considered alternative options or ideas?

☐ What is influencing my opinion right now?

☐ What is another way to look at this situation?

☐ What questions can I ask to follow up, or what facts can I ask about?

☐ Did my mind or opinion change because of this information? Why or why not?

Write these questions down on a piece of paper and keep the list handy so you can refer to it the next time someone gives you new information.

Challenge Yourself!

A comfort zone is a place, thing, or person that makes you feel at ease. For me, my comfort zone is being at the kitchen table with my whole family. Draw a picture of things in your comfort zone that involve zero risk, and think about how they make you feel. Now, imagine what would happen if you *never* stepped outside of that zone. What do you think you might be missing out on?

Your space to doodle and draw!

Challenge Yourself!

Think about what you may be like five years from now. How have you changed? Write a letter to your future self. What do you want your five-year-older self to know? What are some things you hope you'll be able to do by then? What do you hope to congratulate yourself on?

Dear Me,

Key Takeaway

Way to go! You have really opened up and are getting to know yourself on a deeper, more personal level. You discovered things you love about yourself, set goals, opened up your mind, learned about your incredible, flexible brain, and got curious! Your mindset can still vary depending on the situation, and it is normal and okay to go back and forth between a growth and fixed mindset. You are doing awesome right now! Give yourself a high five. You should be extremely proud of you!

> "Every day brings a chance for you to draw in a breath, kick off your shoes, and step out and dance."
>
> —Oprah Winfrey

Your Confident Spark

Facing new situations, people, places, and activities can be scary. When scared or nervous, your body sometimes goes into "shutdown" mode and doesn't help you move forward or face the fear. Your heart might beat faster, you may start sweating or shaking, or your stomach can feel upset. When this happens, it's up to you to *change your mind*.

When you change your mind about a strong fear or nerves, it changes how your body responds and moves it into action. Believing in yourself can make anything possible! But the only way to get yourself geared up for your goal is to make sure the story you are telling yourself is of a brave, confident, and loving girl. The stories you tell yourself, and having a positive outlook, can transform your potential. The only person you can count on in this world to always show up for you is you. And you're worth it!

In the Face of Danger

It is totally normal to shut down when something feels scary. We may even revert to our younger selves and want to curl up and hide. When you embrace your growth mindset, you will find that facing things that are scary, even in small incremental steps, will seem easier. You will need to do the hard work to stay in that mindset, but you and your mind are powerful.

What are you most afraid of? (Because this can be a scary thing to put down in writing, maybe pick a fun color so it doesn't feel quite as scary).

....

....

....

....

We sometimes forget to breathe when we get scared. Trace the box with your writing utensil and follow the breathing prompts: *breathe in for 4 seconds, hold for 4 seconds, breathe out for 4 seconds, hold for 4 seconds.* Next time you find yourself a little nervous or scared, try this box breathing trick! Now, draw your own square and practice on one of the free drawing pages.

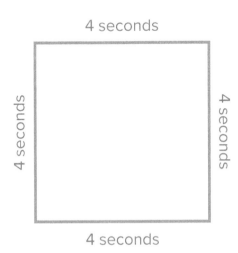

Check the things below that you can use when feeling scared. Add your own ideas to the list.

- ☐ Talking to a trusted grown-up, friend, or sibling
- ☐ Holding someone's hand or asking for a hug
- ☐ Squeezing a stuffed animal
- ☐ Listening to music

- ☐ Using the square breathing exercise
- ☐ Singing or talking to yourself out loud
- ☐ ....
- ☐ ....

Describe a time when fear got in the way of starting or completing something you used to do all the time (without fear).

....
....
....

When trying a new activity, are you usually more scared of the process itself or the outcome?

....
....
....

Are you afraid of what others may think of you? Self-image is something all girls worry about at one point or another. What image of yourself do you think the world sees?

Would you change it?

....

....

....

Who can you turn to when you are afraid?

....

....

....

....

How can this person or people help you move through your fear?

....

....

....

Draw a picture of you being your bravest self.

"Don't worry. It's OK to fall sometimes. And I'm just going to get back up and push even harder."

—Sky Brown

Many girls struggle to see how powerful and beautiful they are. Look at your thinking patterns and analyze where you spend your brain's energy. Is it on the positive? Is it on the negative? These questions will help you identify places to work on to build confidence and live in your true, authentic self.

Copy the following statements. Consider using color, glitter, a fun handwriting/font, etc. Get creative!

I am BRAVE.

....

I am LOVABLE.

....

I can do HARD THINGS.

....

I BELONG here.

....

I am BEAUTIFUL.

....

How does being confident change your attitude?

....

....

....

Did you know you can build confidence just by *trying* something that seems difficult or intimidating? Write down a food or kind of clothing you thought you'd hate but loved once you tried it out. (Proof of confidence!)

....

....

....

Close your eyes and imagine feeling extra confident when making a new friend. If you could do or say anything, what would it be?

....

....

....

....

Pep talks from others (or yourself!) can help you get in the right mindset to take on something with confidence. Write down your best pep talk to yourself.

....

....

....

Use your *voice*! If something is bothering you, or you don't want to "go with the flow," what is something you can say to your friends?

....

....

....

....

Praise yourself for your efforts, not just the outcome. Write down three ways to tell yourself you are proud of how far you have come already.

1. ....

2. ....

3. ....

Make a list of three things you can do now, or want to learn, that some people may incorrectly think aren't "girl" things, like skateboarding or starting a band.

1. ....

2. ....

3. ....

Being brave means having the courage to say your truth. Can you think of a time when you changed your plans or mind because you were afraid of what someone else would think? What could you have said instead?

....

....

....

Don't be afraid to disappoint other people; what you don't want to do is let *yourself* down. I know this is extremely hard as a girl, because we are taught to be people pleasers. Write down three ways that you will not abandon who you are to make other people happy.

1. ....

2. ....

3. ....

> ## "Being successful isn't about being impressive, it's about being inspired."
> ~Michelle Obama

Flipping It Around

The way we see things, or our perception of things, is more important in helping frame our mindset than the actual thing itself. When we reframe, we are changing the connection between our own thoughts, feelings, and behaviors. And although we cannot control the world around us, we *can* control how we think about our thoughts and feel our feelings.

Practice flipping around, or reframing, these events into moments of gratitude. For example, "Oh no, I have a spelling quiz today!" can become "I get to go to school today with all my friends, and I get to take a quiz to see how much I know."

"Ugh, it's raining outside again!"

....

....

"I am so tired. I don't want to do homework."

....

....

"Why do we have to go to Grandma's for dinner tonight?"

....

....

"I hate my clothes. I don't look good in anything today!"

....

....

Describe the last time you felt "stuck" in a negative emotion or in negative self-talk.

....

....

....

....

What helps you get unstuck from negative self-talk?

....

....

....

....

Asking questions and asking for help is proof of a growth mindset. When have you reached out for help instead of persevering alone through something tough?

....

....

....

Failure is going to happen, but redefining winning can make it not feel so bad. Think of a time when you lost or didn't achieve what you wanted. How can you redefine winning? For example, "I may have lost this game of checkers, but I did get to spend the last 30 minutes of uninterrupted time with my sister."

....

....

....

When was the last time you felt disappointed in yourself? How can you go back and redefine winning?

....

....

....

"Filling your cup" means taking care of yourself and keeping your own cup full so that you have enough to give others. Fill the cup below with ways you can make yourself happy and keep your cup full. Examples include calling a friend, creating quiet time, drawing, and practicing yoga.

Here are some strategies to try when you're sad or embarrassed. Add in some of your own ideas!

☐ Write my thought/ plans down

☐ Tell a trusted friend or grown-up

☐ Talk to myself out loud

☐ Send a (positive!) text or email to myself

☐ Make something creative to express myself (baking, drawing, etc.)

☐ Build a music playlist that expresses how I feel

☐ ....

☐ ....

We have all taken a wrong turn, literally and figuratively. Sometimes those wrong turns lead to dead ends. Sometimes we end up in a place we never thought we would be—and it's beautiful. Think of a time when you made a "wrong turn," such as choosing between two places to sit for lunch, or simply walking down the sidewalk. Where did it lead you? Did you discover something new?

....

....

....

....

> "When we live afraid to fail, we don't take risks. We don't bring our entire selves to the table—so we end up failing before we even begin."
>
> —Abby Wambach

This Calls for a Celebration!

That person in the mirror? She is worthy of
celebration! Don't look at who she might be
in the future or who she was yesterday. This
person—you, right now—deserves a pat on
the back! There may be parts of you that you'd
like to change, but accepting and honoring
the person you are *right now* will support your
continued growth mindset journey.

You don't have to prove to *anyone* that you are worthy. Write a congratulations note to yourself for being the fabulous person you are today.

....

....

....

A value is a belief or way of being that is most important to you. Look at the list below and circle your top two most important values. If you don't see your top values, write them in!

balance   beauty   belonging   caring

confidence   creativity   curiosity   fairness

faith   family   freedom   friendship   grace

generosity   health   home   hope   joy

kindness   love   loyalty   nature   openness

patience   peace   teamwork   trust   safety

self-respect   security   wisdom

....

....

Are you surprised by which two value choices you circled? Why or why not?

....

....

Write a sentence about why your top values are important to you. Remember, your definition of your values will differ from other people's definition or meaning of those words.

....

....

....

....

How do you define being "successful" in your values?

....

....

....

....

What is your favorite way to celebrate an achievement or special occasion? Do you like to celebrate with friends and family, or do you prefer to celebrate alone, in private?

....

....

....

....

As we tackled earlier, large goals need to be rewarded for the many steps it takes to get there. Think of smaller rewards you can give yourself for making progress, like the ones below. Circle the ones you like the best!

stickers   extra free time

high fives from a grown-up or friend

electronic/computer time   tasty treats

new pencils or markers or fun erasers

extra time with a friend   read new book

play new board game   new hairstyle

Celebrating or rewarding yourself can help motivate you. Think of three milestones you have coming up and assign specific rewards you want to "work for" or "earn" for accomplishing them. For example: After I study and get a good grade on my next language test, I want to go out for ice cream!

1. ....

2. ....

3. ....

"I'm willing to speak up.
I'm willing to keep going.
I'm willing to listen to what
others have to say.
I'm willing to be my biggest
bestest most powerful self."

—Emma Watson

Carry On and Persist!

Grit! Perseverance! Tenacity! You might not feel like you possess all these qualities, but I am here to tell you that you do. They might be deep down and not ready to come out of you yet, and that is okay. When you are ready to be courageous and take a risk, those qualities will be available to you. Of course, you will have setbacks. You will fail. And you will fall. (Everyone does!) Your growth mindset will be ready to affect how you act when those things happen.

Are you afraid of failure? Why or why not?

....

....

....

....

Have you been protected from disappointment? Or can you identify a recent time where you could have felt disappointed but didn't?

....

....

....

....

When you have a long-term goal, or something that will take longer than a couple weeks to accomplish, do you tend to follow through or give up?

....

....

....

....

Circle the feelings that are true for you when you give up:

sad mad angry embarrassed defeated

fine content uncertain shy indecisive

resentful depressed

Circle all the emotions you feel when you follow through on a goal or long-term project:

glad content joyful confident hesitant

energized motivated inspired determined

creative bold empowered doubtful unsure

proud tired resentful

Are you currently struggling with something or a relationship with someone? What is it, and what could you try that might work better?

....
....
....
....

Perseverance is really, really hard. It can be uncomfortable to face something that feels like it might end up being a mistake or a failure. Acknowledging that it is difficult is the first step. Think of a time when you thought about giving up. How did you pull yourself out of that feeling and keep going?

....

....

....

....

Finding meaning and value in your long-term goals can help you reach them. Looking back to your two most important values, how can you use them to avoid quitting after hitting setbacks?

....

....

....

Have you ever taken the easy way out of things? We know that this doesn't make the challenge or feeling go away. Next time you are thinking of taking the easy way out, what can you do instead?

....

....

....

Write down a phrase, quote, or song lyric that can help you be resilient, such as "Everything will be okay in the end, and if it is not okay, it is not the end." —John Lennon

....

....

....

"I don't like to lose—at anything—yet I've grown most not from victories, but setbacks."

—Serena Williams

Challenge Yourself!

Find an empty jar or shoebox and label it "I am proud of me." Put a pen and some paper or a notepad next to it. Every time you accomplish something during your day, big or small, write it on a small piece of paper and put it in your box. This could be something as small as remembering to be grateful instead of frustrated, or something big like winning an award. At the end of the week, take out all the papers. Read them out loud to yourself or share them with someone special.

Challenge Yourself!

Let's take a quick true/false quiz about grit!

1. If you are an introvert, you cannot have grit. **T** or **F**

2. Grit is important because it helps you succeed. **T** or **F**

3. Grit helps you when you need to persevere to meet long-term goals. **T** or **F**

4. When you face obstacles and you don't give up, you've got grit. **T** or **F**

5. If you are not passionate about something, it is easy to have grit and get through it. **T** or **F**

Answers: 1. F, 2. T, 3. T, 4. T, 5. F

If you didn't get them all correct, that is okay! Go back and think about what led you to your answers.

Challenge Yourself!

Look back to your values on page 53. Think of a time when you had to make a decision or complete a challenge that was extra difficult for you, and your values came into play. What led you to your decision or action? Draw a picture of yourself living one or both of your values on one of the free drawing pages.

Challenge Yourself!

What are you passionate about? What good things do you want to happen? Time to create a vision board! You will need a sheet of poster board, magazines, newspapers, crayons or markers, glue, scissors, glitter, stickers, etc. Cut out, glue, draw, write, and decorate your vision board with things you want to happen and sayings that inspire you to persevere. Turn those dreams into a reality!

Key Takeaway

Now that you have seen your beautiful self, learned to reframe your thinking, and faced your fears and the barriers to your success, how confident do you feel in your ability to make decisions and go after your goals, on a scale of 1 to 10? I hope you have picked out one way to celebrate yourself as you meet those goals! Your perseverance and grit make you unstoppable. You are amazing!

> "If you're comfortable with yourself and know yourself, you're going to shine and radiate, and other people are going to be drawn to you."
>
> —Dolly Parton

Your space to doodle and draw!

Your Endless Potential

In this chapter, you will not only learn to embrace your mistakes and imperfections, but also get excited about the opportunities they offer you. Get ready to get messy! You are perfectly imperfect, just like me, and every other girl out there . . . It's about time you embrace it!

Mistakes Are Normal

From a very young age, we are taught that success is rewarded, and failure is punished. The negative emotions associated with failure can be too big for us to feel, and therefore we avoid the whole thing all together. The feedback we get from others is important; we need to practice accepting it, even when we might not necessarily agree with it. Now is the time to reframe this fear of failure. Let's take a closer look and find purpose in your failures.

What happened the last time you were given negative feedback?

....

....

....

....

Do you challenge negative feedback or listen openly?

....

....

....

....

Would your close friends and family describe you as open to feedback?

....

....

....

....

Did you know that asking for feedback is a great step forward in embracing a growth mindset? Being open to feedback is a sure way to improve! How would you ask your grown-ups for feedback?

....

....

....

....

Failure and mistakes happen, but they don't define who you are. They happen to everybody! What was the last BIG mistake you made?

....

....

....

....

What did you do to correct or learn from this mistake?

....

....

....

....

Have you ever thought "I'm not smart enough," or "What's the point?" after making a mistake? Check off the responses that you are comfortable using as a response to your next mistakes (they'll happen!):

- ☐ Apologize
- ☐ Say what I learned from the mistake
- ☐ Try again
- ☐ Ask for help
- ☐ Ask a question
- ☐ Move on to the next thing

Mistakes are *normal* and essential to learning! Look at them as a form of feedback, letting you know you have something to learn. If your last big mistake could talk, what would it tell you?

....

....

....

....

Have you watched your parents, grandparents, siblings, or other family members make mistakes? How did they respond to those mistakes?

....

....

Look at the examples below. How can you take these situations and redefine failure as a learning experience? 1. You messed up on a science quiz, even though you actually knew the answer. 2. Your teacher asked for volunteers, and even though you really wanted to partic-ipate, you didn't raise your hand. 3. After a conversation with a friend, you reflect on what you said and think, "Why did I say that?"

1. ....

2. ....

3. ....

"Be messy and complicated and afraid and show up anyways."

—Glennon Doyle

Your Perfectly Imperfect Self

Trying to be "perfect" is absolutely exhausting. Know why? Because perfection is unattainable. You know what isn't? Winning! That is why we need to constantly be redefining "winning." The way *you* define a win is the only thing that should matter. Redefining what it means for you will let you embrace your perfectly imperfect self. You are a worthy winner no matter what transpires!

What is one goal that constantly frustrates you?

....

....

....

....

Is it frustrating because you think it is unattainable?

....

....

....

....

How can you take that goal and redefine winning?

....

....

....

....

Striving for perfection can be dangerous. You may think being "perfect" allows you to avoid judgment, blame, or the scary feelings that come with making mistakes. Think of someone you know (personally or not) who you find "perfect." Describe their characteristics here:

....

....

....

....

What makes them *seem* that way to you?

....

....

....

Being a "people pleaser" is a slippery slope into per-fectionistic thinking. Moving from people pleasing to self-acceptance is a way out! Write down one way you can move toward self-acceptance by redefining your ver-sion of "being perfect."

....

....

....

Tell yourself you are already perfect using three positive adjectives, such as funny or kind.

I AM ....

I AM ....

I AM ....

Think of one way that you self-criticize. Now, rethink the thought and rewrite it using self-kindness. Perhaps instead of harping on yourself for being messy, for example, you can compliment yourself on being a creative thinker who isn't bothered by small things.

....

....

....

....

Make a list of the top 10 beautiful ways you are perfectly imperfect.

1. ....

2. ....

3. ....

4. ....

5. ....

6. ....

7. ....

8. ....

9. ....

10. ....

"If you can dance and be free
and not be embarrassed,
you can rule the world."

—Amy Poehler

Figuring It Out!

When presented with a challenge or a problem to solve, try taking a new look at or rethinking your solutions. A simple change in the way you phrase the problem can help you learn more about it. It might be much easier to come to a solution. If you feel you have hit a road-block, put the problem down and come back to it later. Instead of "I give up," try saying "Let me think about this by using some of the strategies I have learned."

Think of and write about a recent social issue you had—maybe a disagreement with a friend or family member.

. . . .

. . . .

. . . .

. . . .

What steps did you take to get to your solution?

. . . .

. . . .

. . . .

. . . .

Did you do it on your own, or with help?

. . . .

. . . .

. . . .

. . . .

Do you think it was your best solution? Why or why not?

....

....

....

....

Let's take a short true/false quiz on what we can do when we need to solve a problem.

1. Staying positive won't help me find a solution. **T** or **F**

2. If I look for what caused the problem, it will likely to lead me to a solution. **T** or **F**

3. If I shy away from problems, I will have a growth mindset. **T** or **F**

4. Looking for resources that can help me might solve my problem faster. **T** or **F**

5. "It will be easier if I do it myself" is always better thinking than asking for help. **T** or **F**

Answers: 1. F, 2. T, 3. F, 4. T, 5. F

When solving a problem, make sure you first identify what it is, figure out what caused it, think about possible solutions, and ask for help when needed! If your solution didn't work, think about what you can learn from the process.

What do you feel makes a person a "problem solver" instead of a complainer?

....

....

....

....

What qualities do you possess that make you a good problem solver?

....

....

....

....

Emotions can run high when you are problem-solving, and this is normal! It is okay to get upset, sad, frustrated, angry, etc. What is your go-to strategy when you are having a big feeling?

....

....

....

Write down a list of three new things you can try when you are feeling frustrated with a problem. For example, listening to music, working out, or calling a friend.

1. ....

2. ....

3. ....

Feel like giving up on something your whole heart is not all that into? It's okay! Try not to fear any judgment or shame that may come with making that hard choice. Is there something you do right now (activity, relationship, etc.) that you are not that into and want to make a change? Write down one way you can start that conversation.

....

....

"Regret doesn't remind us that we did badly. It reminds us that we know we can do better."

—Kathryn Schulz

Trying and Doing

YET This little word can literally change your life! There are some things you need to work at to achieve, and there are some things that come naturally. The skills you don't quite have right now, you don't have . . . **YET.** Using this simple three-letter word can move you from a fixed mindset to a growth mindset. It's not what you can't do or don't know; it's what you can't do or don't know *yet*.

What is one thing you did today or this week that was challenging?

....

....

....

Pay attention to your negative self-statements. Now, take three of those statements and add "YET." For example, "I cannot do this math problem . . . yet."

1. ....

2. ....

3. ....

The first step in holding the power to change your mind is believing you can. Check the box next to these statements if you honestly agree with them:

☐ My beliefs about myself can change.

☐ My beliefs about my abilities can change.

☐ I am the only one who can change them.

☐ I can change my views *now* (not next week, next month, but now).

☐ If I don't like my beliefs after I change them, I can change them again!

Don't worry if you haven't checked all the boxes . . . yet! You'll get there!

List all the times you use "yet" over the next few days:

....

....

....

....

....

Are there certain situations or activities where you are *more* likely to use "yet"? What are they?

....

....

....

Are there certain situations or activities where you are *less* likely to use "yet"? What are they?

....

....

....

....

When you see that your friends are able to do something on the first try and you can't, how can you talk to yourself in a positive and kind way using the power of "yet"?

···
···
···

Write down some barriers or roadblocks you may experience when you feel like you can't use "yet" as a growth mindset strategy, such as lack of sleep or feeling hungry.

···
···
···

Being honest with yourself about your mindset is important. Some days you won't be feeling it. Recognizing it is the first step to turning it around. How can you remind yourself to say "time for a reset" out loud when feeling a fixed mindset?

···
···
···
···

"All of us have to learn how to invent our lives, make them up, imagine them. We need to be taught these skills; we need guides to show us how. If we don't, our lives get made up for us by other people."

—Ursula K. Le Guin

Practice Doesn't Make Perfect, but It Does Make You Better!

What makes you good at something? That's right, practice! To conquer your own mind-set, you have to go all in. Detach yourself from any outcome and enjoy the process in and of itself. You have the power to choose intentional thoughts about yourself and your dreams. Those positive thoughts need positive actions, and both those positive thoughts and actions need practice!

Think of and write down a positive self thought, like "I am really good at puzzles." Then, write down how that thought makes you feel.

Positive thought: ....

How this makes me feel: ....

Think of and write down a negative self thought, like "I will never be good at painting." Then, write down how that thought makes you feel.

Negative thought: ....

How this makes me feel: ....

Take your negative thought or statement and connect it to a new, positive thought instead. Consider using "yet" or turning it around. For example, "I am not good at painting . . . yet." Or, "I really enjoy the feeling of brushing paint on canvas."

....

....

....

....

Practice positive self-talk and making positive self-statements. The more you practice, the more your brain will automatically go to the positive instead of the negative! Write in as many positive statements as you can fit!

....

....

....

....

How does your whole body feel when you practice saying nice things to yourself?

My hands feel: ....

My face feels: ....

My torso/body feel: ....

My legs feel: ....

My heart feels: ....

My head feels: ....

Work on your "practicing muscle" by doing simple tasks regularly, like turning the lights off when you leave the room or throwing your clothes in the dirty laundry. Make a list of the things you can practice that are easy to achieve so you can build your mindfulness around your successful, regular, everyday behaviors.

1. ....

2. ....

3. ....

4. ....

5. ....

What outcomes have you seen from walking away from something that you really wanted to do?

....

....

....

....

Pick a saying or mantra to write down and post where you can see it every day for when you need a reminder to keep practicing a specific goal you want to achieve.

....

....

....

....

When you feel good about yourself, you are more likely to be successful. What are you so-so at that you could do better with a little practice?

....

....

....

....

What is your definition of practice?

....

....

....

....

Challenge Yourself!

Asking for help can be hard! Looking at the following examples, circle Y for yes or N for no if you would feel comfortable asking for help. Then write down how you might ask for help.

Asking a teacher to repeat something because you missed it the first time. **Y** or **N**

....

....

Asking your grown-ups for advice about a friendship issue. **Y** or **N**

....

....

....

Asking your friend to help you with a problem with your grown-ups. **Y** or **N**

....

....

....

Asking a trusted adult for advice about what you should do in a tricky situation. **Y** or **N**

....

....

....

Asking your coach or teacher for extra time or help practicing a skill. **Y** or **N**

....

....

....

"I proved to myself that
I could do things
that I didn't think I could."

—Simone Biles

Challenge Yourself!

For this activity, you will need a packet of sticky notes and a pen or pencil. For the next week, each time you catch yourself using a negative self-statement, write the thought down on a sticky note and add a "YET." Put each sticky note up in your room or house somewhere. At the end of the week, tally up your sticky YETs. How many did you collect?

Challenge Yourself!

In the following chart, fill out at least five things you cannot do . . . YET. Add ways you can get there, then finish with the reason you can do it.

Thing I cannot do . . . YET	Some ways I can get there	Because I can . . .

Challenge Yourself!

Perfectionism and striving to do your best are not the same thing. Look inward the next time you make a decision. Ask yourself, "What did I learn from this? How do I feel about this?" and not "What will other people think?" Follow the flowchart to find how perfectionism impacts you!

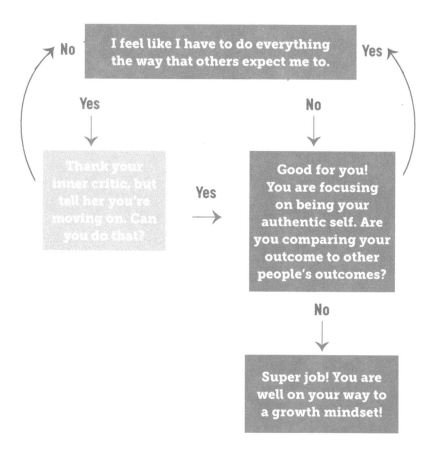

No

I feel like I have to do everything the way that others expect me to.

Yes

Yes

No

Thank your inner critic, but tell her you're moving on. Can you do that?

Yes →

Good for you! You are focusing on being your authentic self. Are you comparing your outcome to other people's outcomes?

No

Super job! You are well on your way to a growth mindset!

Key Takeaway

Look at you go! Your confidence is increasing and you're recognizing what it means to have a growth mindset. You may already have one!

Everything you are writing and reading about here is helping your brain make incredible new connections and, with practice, your neurons will make those connections faster. This means thinking positively will become easier.

With the strategies you've learned, I hope you feel better about making mistakes, embracing your perfect imperfections, evaluating possible solutions, using your "YETs," and remembering to practice! I can tell you from experience that I *still* have to practice my growth mindset when things are scary or when I have to face new problems. It's a constant journey!

"The thing that is really hard, and really amazing, is giving up on being perfect and beginning to work on becoming yourself."

—Anna Quindlen

Your space to doodle and draw!

Your Endless Potential   105

Your Exciting World

Scientists have found that having compassion for others increases your psychological well-being, emotional regulation, and social connections to others. Compassion is also something you can always practice and improve—including compassion for yourself! We all have a natural tendency to have compassion for others, but everyday stressors and life experiences can impact our ability to show ourselves that same compassion.

Making these connections in the brain by practicing self-kindness and compassion for others will help you continue to build your growth mindset. Removing your inner critic is the key to self-compassion. Time to show yourself (and then others) your beautiful, innate kindness!

Together WE CAN!

We are going to shift from a "me" to a "we" mentality for a moment. Everyone—not just you—is on this journey to grow and develop. We are all working on becoming the best versions of ourselves that we can be!

Reading other people's emotions helps us work together better. Label the faces with the emotion they are displaying.

. . . .

Imagine students working in groups in a class; one student has their head on their crossed arms on their desk as the others look on. How do you think this group member feels?

....

....

If you disagreed with this group member, what could you do to help them?

....

....

....

....

How can you do a better job communicating your perspective the next time you and a friend have a misunderstanding about your differing points of view?

. . . .

. . . .

. . . .

. . . .

Embracing a healthy sense of competition can help you face challenges. List some activities you enjoy that are competitive, such as team sports, spelling bees, or elite choir.

. . . .

. . . .

. . . .

. . . .

When you lose at one of these activities, how do you feel?

. . . .

Next time you lose, try asking yourself, "How did the winner win, and what can I learn from this to do better next time?"

Did you know playing games in a friendly, competitive way can actually help increase your self-esteem and social behavior? List a few of your favorite games to play with friends or family.

....

....

....

An aggressive competitor doesn't always make for an aggressive person. It's possible to be an aggressive competitor and a good friend! How do you define the difference?

....

....

....

....

Competing with others effectively is not only healthy, but it also helps you self-advocate and speak up! But not all aggressive competition is beneficial. Is there any unhealthy competition going on right now that you might need to change?

....

....

....

....

Working together is the opposite of competition, whether you're part of a club or packing for a family vacation. What are seven ways you can work well with others?

1. ....

2. ....

3. ....

4. ....

5. ....

6. ....

7. ....

"There is nothing I would not do for those who are really my friends. I have no notion of loving people by halves; it is not my nature."

—Jane Austen

BeYOUtiful

Comparing yourself to others is guaranteed to make you feel bad about yourself. We do this often without even noticing. Bringing an awareness to your thoughts and your reactions to others can help you stop this habit. Once you start to go down the path of comparison, stop, take a breath, and try to practice gratitude instead.

You have some amazing qualities! What are three great things you've done since yesterday?

1. ....

2. ....

3. ....

Jealousy is actually a feeling about yourself, not the other person. Write about how changing your perspective can help eliminate feelings of jealousy.

....

....

....

....

What is something someone has that you want?

....

....

....

....

Why do you want it?

....

What would you do if you had it?

....

How would you feel if you had it?

....

If jealousy is taking you down a path that you don't want to go down, what are three things you can do to move on from that feeling? Some suggestions include turning and walking away or journaling.

1. ....

2. ....

3. ....

Falling into the trap of comparing yourself to others prevents you from moving forward. This may sound in your head like, "Well, because I am not as good as them, I should quit now because I am never going to get better." How can you take this thought, this fixed mindset, and turn it into a growth mindset?

....

....

....

....

Looking at someone else's success as motivation to try harder and do better will retrain your brain to step up and pursue your goals! Who in your life right now inspires you to do more and keep going?

....

....

....

....

Thinking of someone you may be jealous of, how can this feeling inspire you to try harder to get what you want? Will you?

....

....

....

....

"We embrace the things that make us unique."

—Janelle Monáe

Quirky Is Cool!

When you appreciate what makes you different, you give yourself permission to push your boundaries and move past what is "expected." When you do that, you open worlds of possibilities for yourself: new experiences, new friends, and new adventures.

A "gut feeling" is your inner voice; if you are calm and quiet enough, you can hear it. When was the last time you had a "gut feeling"? What did you end up doing?

....

....

....

Write down one thing that you hide from the world because you are worried that it may be viewed as quirky or "different."

....

....

....

....

Think about two ways to let your quirkiness out into the world!

1. ....

....

2. ....

....

How do you think other people (who you love and respect) will respond to it?

....

....

....

....

The world is making strides to be more inclusive, but it is far from perfect. What is a positive way you can reframe "standing out" for those who you may view as being different from you?

....

....

....

....

What makes them unique?

....

....

....

....

Honoring your own uniqueness will increase your self-confidence and creativity. Next to each word, write the first personal characteristic that comes to mind:

Special: ....

Funny: ....

Different: ....

One of a kind: ....

Have you previously held back from letting your true self come out because you were afraid of what others would think?

....

....

....

....

Let yourself shine! In the spaces around the sun, write down five ways you want to show the world what you're made of. What are your top five "rays of sunshine" you want to spread to those around you?

"You can have fun and have purpose, be respectful and speak your mind."

~Beyoncé

Being Kind to Others

Offering kindness to others means being respectful, caring, inclusive, and courageous, and taking responsibility for our behavior. Scientists have found that showing kindness to others stimulates a part of our brain that cultivates our social-emotional skills and supports our growth mindset.

One of the hardest times to offer kindness is when you feel someone has wronged you or when they have hurt your feelings. Other people's behavior and emotions are not our responsibility, only our own are, so we are in control here! Showing kindness to those who hurt us not only helps us feel better about ourselves, but it also allows our wonderfulness to shine bright.

What does the word *kindness* mean to you?

....

....

....

....

Think about a time you made someone else feel happy. Maybe you held the door for someone or picked something up that they had dropped. Write how that made you feel.

....

....

....

....

Think about a time when someone else made you feel happy. Write about what they did and how it made you feel.

....

....

....

....

How do you know when someone is showing you kindness?

....

....

....

....

How are you kind to your own mind, body, and heart?

Mind: ....

Body: ....

Heart: ....

Action bank:

offer a compliment   **hold the door**   pick up litter

make a card   run an errand for someone

help out in the kitchen   give a homemade gift

do a chore without being asked   clean your room

send a positive text   walk someone else's dog

In the following chart, use the terms in the action bank on page 126 (or write your own!) and sort the acts of kindness that you "have done" or "would like to do."

Have Done	Would Like to Do

It is normal to feel anger when someone hurts our feelings, but it is not okay to be stuck there. We need to find our compassion and forgiveness, and eventually move on. What is one possible reason this person may have hurt your feelings?

....

....

....

....

Write down something unpleasant in their own life that might have caused them to behave that way toward you. This is not an excuse for their behavior but an acceptance on your part.

....

....

....

....

You don't have to like this person or be friends with them, but kindness may change their behavior toward you. No need to focus on who was right and who was wrong. How can you show this person kindness and forgiveness?

....

....

....

Time to move on! Your positive energy will continue to spread as you share your kindness. Share some traits and characteristics you want to be recognized for when you grow up.

....

....

....

....

"No one can make you feel inferior without your consent."

—Eleanor Roosevelt

R-E-S-P-E-C-T: Find Out What It Means to YOU

What does it mean to respect yourself? Appreciating who you are and what you have to offer is one of the best ways to honor yourself. It means being proud of your value, skills, opinions, knowledge, talents, and gifts. It allows you to feel comfortable not being perfect, and to forgive yourself for any mistakes you make. Holding yourself in high regard demonstrates how you want to be treated by other people.

Taking care of your own needs sets boundaries with those around you. Write your top five ways to show yourself respect. Some examples include exercising, long bubble baths, and kind self-talk.

1. ....

2. ....

3. ....

4. ....

5. ....

Saying "no" helps let people know what is and is not okay with you. Learning to do this will make you stronger! What have you recently said "yes" to when you really wanted to say "no"?

....

....

How could you say "no" in a positive way (for instance, explaining your boundaries)?

....

....

....

Surrounding yourself with positive people and influences will have a healthy impact on your self-image and may affect your everyday decisions. List five people or things that positively influence your life and make it better.

1. ....

2. ....

3. ....

4. ....

5. ....

Keeping emotions bottled up can be detrimental! When have you recently experienced an extreme emotion, such as anger, sadness, or embarrassment? Write about it as if you were telling your closest friend how you were feeling.

....

....

....

Think about that feeling. Draw a picture of yourself that includes your facial expression and body language. Now close your eyes and think about what you see, smell, touch, and taste. Paying attention to these details may help you express your emotional state.

Write a love letter to your body that tells all the reasons you love and respect it.

Dear Body,

When others are speaking, show respect by listening actively before forming opinions or thinking about what you are going to say next. What could you do to show someone you are actively listening while they are speaking?

....

....

....

A simple "Thank you" or "Thank you for trusting me with this information" might be the best way to respond when someone tells you something important. You don't always need to offer your opinion or thoughts. Write how you could respond to a friend to show them respect:

- "My cousin is moving, and I am super upset."

....

- "I don't know how to tell my mom I broke her flower vase."

....

- "My pet is sick."

....

- "I don't want to go to dance class anymore."

....

When others make a mistake, calling them out in front of a bunch of people is embarrassing (right?). It's better to take them aside and mention it. How could you tell someone they made a mistake without making a big deal about it?

....

....

....

"When one door of happiness closes, another opens; but often we look so long at the closed door that we do not see the one which has been opened for us."

—Helen Keller

Challenge Yourself!

Imagine a picture of yourself working with a team of people to achieve a single outcome.
    Now answer the following questions:

What are you working on?

....

....

....

How will you achieve this outcome?

....

....

Challenge Yourself!

Take this short true/false quiz!

1. Understanding and reading other people's emotions will help me be a better team player. **T** or **F**

2. Feeling jealous is the other person's fault. T or F

3. Comparing myself to others may trap me in a fixed mindset. **T** or **F**

4. Being different is bad. **T** or **F**

5. I need to let the world see who I truly am (and I need to let my kindness shine). **T** or **F**

Answers: 1. T, 2. F, 3. T, 4. F, 5. T

If you didn't get all the answers correct, that is okay! You are still learning and practicing—which is a part of your growth mindset!

Challenge Yourself!

Write five little-known facts about yourself. Then, interview a family member or best friend for five little-known facts about them. It is fun to learn new things about the people you love!

1. ....

2. ....

3. ....

4. ....

5. ....

1. ....

2. ....

3. ....

4. ....

5. ....

Challenge Yourself!

When you started writing in this journal, you were at the very beginning of your growth mindset journey. Now that you have made it to the end, rate yourself (honestly!) on a scale of 1 to 10 on how confident and comfortable you are with the following:

1. I can acknowledge and embrace my imperfections. ....

2. I can view challenges and mistakes as opportunities. ....

3. I can use the word "yet" for things I cannot do. ....

4. I can enjoy the process and the journey without worrying about the outcome. ....

5. I can celebrate successes and wins with myself and with others. ....

6. I can reward my actions and not outcomes. ....

7. I can persist and use my grit. ....

8. I can redefine winning and make new goals. ....

9. I can take risks. ....

10. I can take responsibility for my thinking and my behavior. ....

It is okay to not feel totally confident in all of these things yet, but give yourself a high five for how great you are doing! We are all still practicing. We can continue this journey together, and you can revisit this journal whenever you want.

Key Takeaway

Another journal section complete! Girl, you are on FIRE! After going through this section, you should feel better about working with and not comparing yourself to others, embracing your own beautiful quirkiness, offering kindness (even when it feels the hardest), and showering yourself with much-earned respect. These are all foundational building blocks to practice so your brain can continue to make lasting connections. Kindness, especially, will support you as you continue to build your growth mindset. These are not easy things to accomplish, and you should absolutely celebrate your success here!

But the most important questions are: Do *you* believe that you are on the path to success? And do *you* believe that with practice you can achieve anything? If the answers are "yes," then watch out world—THIS BRAVE GIRL'S GOT GRIT and a GROWTH MINDSET!

"What sets you apart can sometimes feel like a burden and it's not. And a lot of the time, it's what makes you great."

–Emma Stone

CONGRATULATIONS!

YOU DID IT! Your journal is complete! Your courage, bravery, creativity, and confidence throughout this journal have all been shining through as you built your growth mindset! How are you feeling about all the new things you learned? Did you uncover new things about yourself? How did you change throughout this process?

Keep this book handy for future use, to go back and work through any pages again to see if you get different answers. You can rework the sections in a notebook or journal. Just as with this book, you can tell those pages anything you want, free of judgment or criticism.

Although this journal is done, your growth mindset journey continues! You will continue to learn a lot about yourself, and others around you, as you become more aware of your mindset and how your thoughts affect your behavior. For now, celebrate all the work you've done so far. You are an amazing girl with a ton of love to share. Fuel your fire with confidence and strength, and get out there and change the world!

MORE SPACE TO DRAW AND WRITE

RESOURCES

Books for Kids

Empowered Girls: Activities and Affirmations for Empowering Strong, Confident Girls by Allison Kimmey

The Girls' Guide to Growth Mindset: A Can-Do Approach to Building Confidence, Courage, and Grit by Kendra Coates

Good Night Stories for Rebel Girls: 100 Tales of Extraordinary Women by Elena Favilli and Francesca Cavallo

Growth Mindset Workbook for Kids: 55 Fun Activities to Think Creatively, Solve Problems, and Love Learning by Peyton Curley

Learn, Grow, Succeed! A Kid's Growth Mindset Journal by Brandy Thompson

The Story of Frida Kahlo by Susan B. Katz

The Story of Malala Yousafzai by Joan Marie Galat

The Story of Simone Biles by Rachelle Burk

Strong Is the New Pretty by Kate T. Parker

Today Is Great! A Daily Gratitude Journal for Kids by Vicky Perreault

Books for Grown-Ups

Fall Down 7 Times, Get Up 8: Raising and Teaching Self-Motivated Learners by Debbie Silver

The Growth Mindset Playbook: A Teacher's Guide to Promoting Student Success by Annie Brock and Heather Hundley

Mindset: The New Psychology of Success by Carol Dweck

ACKNOWLEDGMENTS

I want to thank the women and girls in my life who helped bring this book to life. My daughter, Wynter, and two sons, Xander and Boden, were constantly on my mind as I wrote.

These preteen years are when the world starts telling you to ignore your inner fire, to stop trusting your gut, and to only focus on and believe what the outside world says. *You* have the power to change the world. *Trust* yourself!

ABOUT THE AUTHOR

Jamie Leigh Bassos, MS, BCBA, is a behavior analyst and has worked with infants, children, and families for over 20 years in classroom, home, and community settings. She received her education and training for individuals with learning differences and behavior disorders from the New England Center for Children. She is currently vice president at Continuum Behavioral Health and lives in South Florida with her husband and three children. When not working or parenting, you can usually find her running races all over the country with her local running club, Moms RUN This Town.

CPSIA information can be obtained
at www.ICGtesting.com
Printed in the USA
BVHW092253280222
630168BV00004B/4